Instant Premium Drupal Themes

Learn how to create visually stunning themes to add the wow factor to all of your Drupal sites!

Pankaj Sharma

BIRMINGHAM - MUMBAI

Instant Premium Drupal Themes

First published: October 2013

Production Reference: 1241013

Published by Packt Publishing Ltd.
Livery Place
35 Livery Street
Birmingham B3 2PB, UK.

ISBN 978-1-78328-175-6

www.packtpub.com

Credits

Author
Pankaj Sharma

Reviewers
Pradeep Saran

Anton Sidashin

Acquisition Editors
Akram Hussain

Andrew Duckworth

Commissioning Editor
Priyanka Shah

Technical Editor
Krishnaveni Haridas

Copy Editor
Kirti Pai

Project Coordinator
Romal Karani

Proofreader
Ting Baker

Production Coordinator
Pooja Chiplunkar

Cover Work
Pooja Chiplunkar

Cover Image
Sheetal Aute

About the Author

Pankaj Sharma is a senior software engineer with a multinational IT firm in Noida, India. He has more than five years of developing experience in Perl, PHP, and CMS (WordPress, Drupal). Besides these technologies, he has also worked on AJAX, JavaScript, MySQL, and PostgreSQL. He has developed scalable websites for some of the world's leading companies in FMCG and the media and entertainment domain. He completed his degree (BSc.) in 2003 and post-graduate Master's degree (MCA) in 2007 in Dehradun. His interests include Cloud Computing and Big Data and his hobbies include writing, reading, travelling, and delving into philosophy.

I would like to express deep gratitude to God, my 'guiding light' and inspiration. I would like to thank my brothers Neeraj Sharma and Dheeraj Sharma for their valuable suggestions and inputs. Thanks to my parents, Mr. and Mrs. Suresh Chand Sharma, as well for their unconditional love and support.

About the Reviewers

Pradeep Saran is the founder of Devsaran (`http://devsaran.com/`), a Bangalore-based software development startup that specializes in developing modern web applications. His primary focus is frontend development and web application development.

He has been very active in the Drupal open source community. He has developed and maintains contributed modules and themes on `drupal.org`. His Drupal user account can be found at `https://drupal.org/user/1031208`.

> I would like to thank my family and friends for their support in all of my endeavors. I would also like to thank Packt Publishing for providing me with the opportunity to do something useful. Thanks also to the Drupal community, whose willingness to share their knowledge and advice has become an invaluable asset.

Anton Sidashin is the CEO and, at the same time, the developer of a small Drupal agency, `Pixeljets.com`, which specializes in building beautiful Drupal projects and themes—both commercial and open source. The core of the agency is Anton and his brother Oleg, and there is also a team of Drupal and Symfony2 ninjas who help these brothers a lot.

He has been working with Drupal since the release of its 4.5 version in 2005, when he fell in love with the flexibility and power of this CMF.

He is a Zend-certified PHP5 engineer and he also worked as the senior architect of CS-Cart 2 e-commerce solutions back in 2007-2008.

www.PacktPub.com

Support files, eBooks, discount offers and more

You might want to visit www.PacktPub.com for support files and downloads related to your book.

Did you know that Packt offers eBook versions of every book published, with PDF and ePub files available? You can upgrade to the eBook version at www.PacktPub.com and as a print book customer, you are entitled to a discount on the eBook copy. Get in touch with us at service@packtpub.com for more details.

At www.PacktPub.com, you can also read a collection of free technical articles, sign up for a range of free newsletters and receive exclusive discounts and offers on Packt books and eBooks.

http://PacktLib.PacktPub.com

Do you need instant solutions to your IT questions? PacktLib is Packt's online digital book library. Here, you can access, read and search across Packt's entire library of books.

Why Subscribe?

- ▸ Fully searchable across every book published by Packt
- ▸ Copy and paste, print and bookmark content
- ▸ On demand and accessible via web browser

Free Access for Packt account holders

If you have an account with Packt at www.PacktPub.com, you can use this to access PacktLib today and view nine entirely free books. Simply use your login credentials for immediate access.

Table of Contents

Preface

This book will describe the relevant steps used to create Drupal themes from raw HTML in a simple and lucid manner and save the energy and time wasted in irrelevant tasks.

What this book covers

Understanding Drupal jargon, covers the commonly used Drupal terminologies that are essential for theme development in Drupal. The heart of Drupal themes and theme engines will also be explained in this chapter.

Understanding Drupal's theme structure (Simple), covers the names of Drupal templates and pages and their meaning/work. Drupal's default themes will be explained here.

Configuring raw HTML in the Drupal environment (Simple), explains how an HTML file is configured in the Drupal environment using the knowledge acquired in the preceding two sections.

Breaking down HTML in parts (Intermediate), explains how to break down HTML regions of Drupal theme such as header, footer, and content.

Populating the Drupal theme with dynamic content (Advanced), *explains* the prerequisites to use Drupal template variables and how to use them.

Theme how tos (Advanced), introduces the commonly used code in Drupal theme development, which will save lot of time and energy.

What you need for this book

To run the examples in the book, the following software will be required:

- ▶ XAMPP or WAMP: `http://www.apachefriends.org/en/xampp-windows.html`
- ▶ Drupal: `https://drupal.org/download`

Who this book is for

This book is useful for developers who are new to Drupal. It's assumed that you have some experience in HTML,PHP, and CSS .Readers are expected to have the PHP (LAMP/WAMP) environment ready and working to install Drupal. It is assumed that the user is aware how to install Drupal. A little bit of familiarity with CMS is also expected from the user. Rest of the things have been taken care of in the book.

Conventions

In this book, you will find a number of styles of text that distinguish between different kinds of information. Here are some examples of these styles, and an explanation of their meaning.

Code words in text are shown as follows: "Go to your theme's `.info` file."

A block of code is set as follows:

```
Code [<?php
if (!$page) {
  print "<h2><a href=\"$node_url\">$title</a></h2>";
}

if ($submitted) {
  print "<span class=\"submitted\">$submitted</span>";
}
?>]
```

New terms and **important words** are shown in bold. Words that you see on the screen, in menus or dialog boxes for example, appear in the text like this: "Click on the **Clear all caches** button located at **Administration | Configuration | Development | Performance**."

 Warnings or important notes appear in a box like this.

Reader feedback

Feedback from our readers is always welcome. Let us know what you think about this book—what you liked or may have disliked. Reader feedback is important for us to develop titles that you really get the most out of.

To send us general feedback, simply send an e-mail to feedback@packtpub.com, and mention the book title via the subject of your message.

If there is a topic that you have expertise in and you are interested in either writing or contributing to a book, see our author guide on www.packtpub.com/authors.

Customer support

Now that you are the proud owner of a Packt book, we have a number of things to help you to get the most from your purchase.

Downloading the example code

You can download the example code files for all Packt books you have purchased from your account at http://www.packtpub.com. If you purchased this book elsewhere, you can visit http://www.packtpub.com/support and register to have the files e-mailed directly to you.

Errata

Although we have taken every care to ensure the accuracy of our content, mistakes do happen. If you find a mistake in one of our books—maybe a mistake in the text or the code—we would be grateful if you would report this to us. By doing so, you can save other readers from frustration and help us improve subsequent versions of this book. If you find any errata, please report them by visiting http://www.packtpub.com/submit-errata, selecting your book, clicking on the **errata submission form** link, and entering the details of your errata. Once your errata are verified, your submission will be accepted and the errata will be uploaded on our website, or added to any list of existing errata, under the Errata section of that title. Any existing errata can be viewed by selecting your title from http://www.packtpub.com/support.

Piracy

Piracy of copyright material on the Internet is an ongoing problem across all media. At Packt, we take the protection of our copyright and licenses very seriously. If you come across any illegal copies of our works, in any form, on the Internet, please provide us with the location address or website name immediately so that we can pursue a remedy.

Please contact us at copyright@packtpub.com with a link to the suspected pirated material.

We appreciate your help in protecting our authors, and our ability to bring you valuable content.

Questions

You can contact us at questions@packtpub.com if you are having a problem with any aspect of the book, and we will do our best to address it.

Instant Premium Drupal Themes

Welcome to *Instant Premium Drupal Themes*. This book will help you to design a Drupal theme from scratch with ease.

This book will make users aware of Drupal terminology and guide them to create a Drupal theme from a raw HTML file.

Understanding Drupal jargon

Before starting to create a Drupal theme, a user should be aware about Drupal and its terminologies. Knowing Drupal jargon will make the journey smooth. Drupal revolves around a 'node, which has a has special meaning in Drupal as it gives rise to other Drupal terminologies.

In this section the user will get to know the meaning of frequently used Drupal terms.

While designing a Drupal theme, we need to understand the following terms:

- **API (Application programming interface)**: API is a set of rules and specifications that needs to be followed by Drupal developers to interact with the Drupal core, such as the theme system, Form API, and Field API.
    - Drupal uses the theme system API for the themes that are located at `includes/theme.inc`.

- **Argument**: An argument is part of the path of a Drupal website, or the path to a Drupal website can be considered to be made of 'arguments'. For example, in the `/node/937` path, the first argument is `node` and the second is `937`.

- ▶ **Article and Basic Page**: Article (also known as Story in the earlier version of Drupal) and Basic page (Page) are the two default content types in Drupal.

  - ❏ Frequently changed content is assigned to the Article content type (for example, News), while static content is assigned to the Basic page content type.

  Click on **Content**. The following screen will appear. Now, click on the link highlighted in yellow:

The following screen displays **Article** and **Basic Page**. These are the two important content types in Drupal. You can say they are nodes actually:

- ▶ **Base theme**: Base themes can be termed as frameworks of the Drupal theme. Some of the popular base themes include Zen, Omega, and AdaptiveTheme. These themes can be reused to create new themes.

You can see all the available themes in Drupal's `themes` folder highlighted in yellow in the following screenshot:

Name	Date modified	Type	Size
includes	28-08-2013 09:54	File folder	
misc	28-08-2013 09:54	File folder	
modules	28-08-2013 09:54	File folder	
profiles	28-08-2013 09:54	File folder	
scripts	28-08-2013 09:54	File folder	
sites	28-08-2013 09:54	File folder	
themes	28-08-2013 09:54	File folder	
.gitignore	08-08-2013 07:34	GITIGNORE File	1 KB
.htaccess	08-08-2013 07:34	HTACCESS File	6 KB
authorize.php	08-08-2013 07:34	PHP File	7 KB
CHANGELOG	08-08-2013 07:34	Text Document	81 KB
COPYRIGHT	08-08-2013 07:34	Text Document	2 KB
cron.php	08-08-2013 07:34	PHP File	1 KB
index.php	08-08-2013 07:34	PHP File	1 KB
INSTALL.mysql	08-08-2013 07:34	Text Document	2 KB
INSTALL.pgsql	08-08-2013 07:34	Text Document	2 KB
install.php	08-08-2013 07:34	PHP File	1 KB
INSTALL.sqlite	08-08-2013 07:34	Text Document	2 KB
INSTALL	08-08-2013 07:34	Text Document	18 KB
LICENSE	18-09-2011 03:20	Text Document	18 KB
MAINTAINERS	08-08-2013 07:34	Text Document	8 KB
README	08-08-2013 07:34	Text Document	6 KB
robots	08-08-2013 07:34	Text Document	2 KB
update.php	08-08-2013 07:34	PHP File	20 KB
UPGRADE	08-08-2013 07:34	Text Document	10 KB
web.config	08-08-2013 07:34	CONFIG File	3 KB

▸ **Region and blocks**: A Drupal theme is divided into regions such as the header, footer, content, left sidebar, and right sidebar. Blocks are assigned to regions. So, blocks are a part of regions. Blocks are the areas visible in the regions.

Examples of blocks are Search Form, User login, and Navigation. If you want to display a Search form in the footer, place the Search form block in the Footer region.

- **Entity**: Entity is any defined chunk of data in Drupal. This includes data such as nodes, users, taxonomy terms, files, and so on. Contributed modules can define custom entities. Each entity type can have multiple bundles.

- **Clean URL**: Drupal allows us to create a clean URL when the `Path` module is enabled (for example, `http://www.example.com/node/83`).

- **Contributed**: This term is used for the themes and modules that are not a part of the Drupal core. They are installed separately to enhance the capability of Drupal.

- **Field**: These are the elements of data that can be attached to a node or other Drupal entities. Fields commonly contain text, image, or terms.

- **Module**: This is the bundle of code written according to Drupal conventions that extend Drupal features and functionality. There are two types of modules, Core and Contributed.

  You can view all the modules in the **Admin** panel as given in the following screenshot:

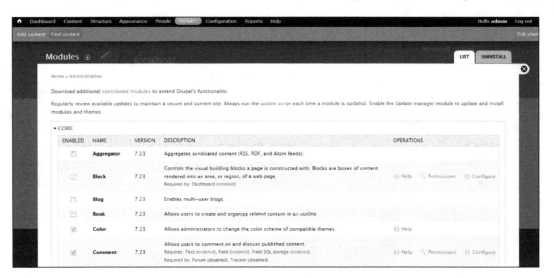

- **Menu**: In Drupal, the term menu refers both to the clickable navigational elements on a page, and Drupal's internal system for handling requests. When a request is sent to Drupal, the menu system uses the provided URL to determine the functions to be called.

- **Node**: Each content in Drupal is a node. Node belongs to the content type. Content type further belongs to taxonomy.

  For example, `http://drupal.org/node/937` tells that a node is having an NID (node id) of 937.

- **Tag/term**, **Taxonomy**, **Vocabulary**: Drupal is a powerful CMS as it revolves around content. Content classification is handled by the powerful **Taxonomy** module. A term is the basis of Drupal's content classification mechanism. A term is the metadata that is applied on a node. A collection of terms is called Vocabulary.

  You can see this part of Drupal in **Admin** by clicking on the **Structure** link as given in the following screenshot:

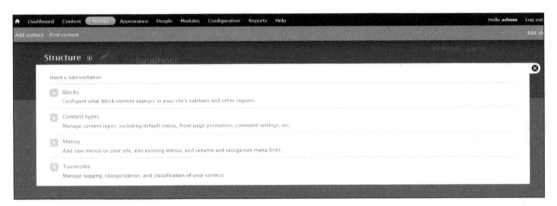

- **Theme engine**: Theme engine is a set of PHP scripts that handles the Drupal theme system. `phptemplate` is the default theme engine, but there are 19 other theme engines, including `Smarty`, that can be configured.

  You can check the theme engine at the following path in Drupal code:

  `/themes/engines.`

▸ **Theme and templates**: A theme is a combination of PHP, INFO, CSS, JPG, GIF, PNG, and HTML, and is responsible for the look and feel of the Drupal website. A theme is a combination of templates. A template is the presentation file where Drupal functions populate data with the help of the theme engine. In simple terms, it's an HTML file having Drupal functions.

This is how a theme looks in Drupal:

images	29-08-2013 22:08	File folder	
ie	08-08-2013 07:34	Cascading Style S...	1 KB
ie6	08-08-2013 07:34	Cascading Style S...	1 KB
ie7	08-08-2013 07:34	Cascading Style S...	1 KB
jquery.ui.theme	08-08-2013 07:34	Cascading Style S...	15 KB
logo	08-08-2013 07:34	PNG image	4 KB
maintenance-page.tpl.php	08-08-2013 07:34	PHP File	2 KB
page.tpl.php	08-08-2013 07:34	PHP File	2 KB
reset	08-08-2013 07:34	Cascading Style S...	3 KB
screenshot	08-08-2013 07:34	PNG image	13 KB
seven.info	08-08-2013 07:47	INFO File	1 KB
style	08-08-2013 07:34	Cascading Style S...	19 KB
style-rtl	08-08-2013 07:34	Cascading Style S...	4 KB
template.php	08-08-2013 07:34	PHP File	5 KB
vertical-tabs	08-08-2013 07:34	Cascading Style S...	3 KB
vertical-tabs-rtl	08-08-2013 07:34	Cascading Style S...	1 KB

▸ **Weight**: Weight means priority in Drupal. A lower weight value (-10) will float at the top of lists, while heavier (+10) weights will appear at the bottom of lists.

Now let's talk about some other options, or some pieces of general information that are relevant to this task.

Drupal theme engines

The theme engine is the heart of Drupal's theme system. Theme engines handle the integration of PHP templates with the Drupal theme system.

By default, the `phptemplate` theme engine is available in Drupal, but the user has the freedom to use other theme engines as well. The `phptemplate` theme engine is faster than other theme engines as template files are written in pure PHP using this theme engine.

There are other main theme engines available, which are as follows:

- **Zengine**: The Zengine theme engine is a CSS-oriented theme engine based entirely on `phptemplate`.

- **Awesomengine**: It is similar to the `phptemplate` theme engine. The power of this theme engine lies in its ability to create dynamic CSS, as PHP code can be embedded in HTML templates and CSS files using this engine.

- **Smarty theme engine**: This is based on the `Smarty` template engine. Smarty is a web template system written in PHP and the objective of Smarty is the separation of the frontend web pages from the backend.

The following is a section with more information relevant to this task, possibly discussing some more options.

Understanding Drupal's theme structure (Simple)

The Drupal theme is located in the `themes` folder in the root. Drupal provides some themes by default such as bartik, garland, seven, and stark.

These themes can be used as a skeleton to create your own theme.

We will use the Garland theme as the base theme to explain Drupal in this book.

Garland's templates will be used as the base.

Any Drupal theme consists of the files mentioned in the *Getting ready* section. These files are needed to create any Drupal theme.

Getting ready

A list of the Drupal theme files and a brief description of their functionalities are discussed in this section.

While creating a Drupal theme, knowledge of each theme file is mandatory. The name of a theme file should not be changed at any cost. Drupal does not understand any other file except its own theme file.

Template name	Template function
`theme-name.info`	This is the gateway of Drupal themes. This file contains information about the theme's name, its version, and its description. Other than this, the theme skeleton is also mentioned here.CSS files are also configured in this file.
`comment.tpl.php`	Comments inside the content are taken care of by this file.
`style.css`	CSS of the site is placed here. Apart from `style.css`, other CSS files can also be used, such as `fix-ie.css`, `fix-ie-rtl.css` (to address browser compatibility issues) and `print.css`.
`page.tpl.php`	This is the main file of the Drupal theme. The Drupal theme revolves around this file. This is pivotal for the development of the Drupal theme.
`node.tpl.php`	This file is responsible for the content of the Drupal node. You can say that the node is governed from here.
`logo.png`	It is optional but it is advised to have this file, since it is according to Drupal conventions and it provides a face to the theme.
`screenshot.png`	A screenshot of your theme is represented by an image and it helps you to recognize your theme in the **Admin** panel.
`template.php`	In this file we can write our own theme function. It is advisable to write theme specific functions here. We should not try to hack the Drupal core as it might disrupt Drupal as a whole.
`theme-settings.php`	Theme settings and global variables can be defined here.
`maintenance-page.tpl`	As the name suggests, this page is displayed when the site is down for maintenance. It's optional, but recommended.
`region.tpl.php`	This template is used to display a region in the Drupal theme.
`block.tpl.php`	This template is used to display blocks in the Drupal theme.
`README.txt`	This file can be used to provide instructions to users.
`html.tpl.php`	This file is used to display the basic HTML structure of a single Drupal page.

How to do it...

We need to perform the following steps:

1. Download the latest version of Drupal from `https://drupal.org/download`
2. Install Drupal (follow the instructions to install Drupal at `https://drupal.org/documentation/install`)
3. Supposing your installation name is `drupal`, go to `garland` in the `themes` folder.
4. You can find all the necessary Drupal templates at `drupal\themes\garlandpath`.

There's more...

Drupal 7 provides listed themes. By and large, all themes contain the above mentioned template files with different directory structures.

The structures of the following default themes can be copied and used to create your own Drupal theme:

- Bartik
- Garland
- Seven
- Stark

Configuring raw HTML in the Drupal environment (Simple)

How to configure a raw HTML file in a Drupal environment will be explained here in brief. Doing this is important as HTML will start displaying when this step will be followed.

Drupal is a CMS that understands everything that has been written as per its API. It is made up of various APIs and the Theme API handles everything about the theme. If a user places HTML files that are having user-defined names, Drupal is not going to understand that.

Filenames of a theme and variables used in themes should be as per the Drupal Theme API.

We will explain in the following section how a raw HTML file is broken into various files and how they are named, so that Drupal understands them and can parse them.

Getting ready

We are taking `garland` as the base theme for all the instructions in the following section (Drupal 7 is being used in all the instructions).

How to do it...

1. Copy the folder of an existing Drupal theme (that is, `garland`) to `sites\all\themes`.

2. Rename the copied theme folder to your theme. Let's suppose the new theme name is `packt`.

3. Follow the directory structure of the old theme (`garland`) in the new theme (`packt`).

4. Rename `garland.info` to `packt.info` and change the details such as the name and description in the file. The moment you complete this step, the theme will be reflected in the **Admin** panel. Rename the `garland` theme's variables as per the new theme.

5. Navigate to **Admin | Appearance**. Your newly created theme should appear in the **Disabled themes** section.

6. Enable the newly created theme (that is, `packt`) and check at the frontend.

7. Start coding in the template files of the new theme as per your requirement and the provided HTML. Refer to the next section for more details.

   The following screenshot explains the file structure of the `garland` theme (all Drupal files will have files with the same name):

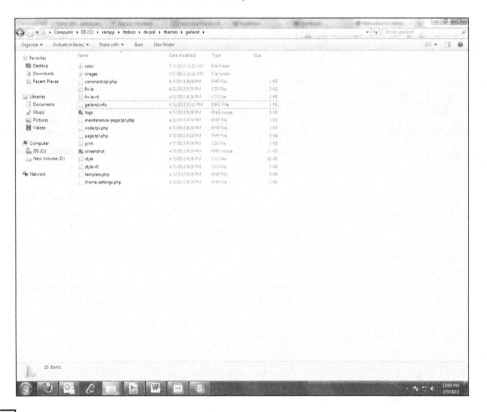

Once our theme is configured successfully in Drupal, it should appear in the **Admin** panel. Our theme, `packt`, is configured successfully as shown in the following screenshot:

Breaking down HTML in parts (Intermediate)

While customizing the Drupal theme, we need to use Drupal's built-in functions and variables.

If there is a need to create theme-specific functions and methods, then that can be done in the `template.php` file located in Drupal's `themes` folder.

Availability of these variables depends on whether they have been enabled in the **Admin** panel or not.

To populate a raw HTML file with dynamic content, you need to use Drupal variables.

These variables can be found at the following link (the user can refer to API to know the details of the Drupal variable):

`https://api.drupal.org/api/drupal/globals/7`

We need to configure the `.info` file. This file has key-value pairs with the keys on the left and the values on the right. Semicolons are used for comments.

The following information is provided in the `.info` file:

- Name of the theme
- Description of the theme
- Version of the theme
- Stylesheet to be used in the template

  You can get more information about the `.info` file at

  `https://drupal.org/node/171205`

How to do it...

We can configure HTML in Drupal by performing the following steps:

1. Break down your HTML code as per the Drupal templates.
2. You need to identify the header, footer, and body part with your HTML code.
3. Configure CSS in the `.info` file. A CSS file will be picked up from this path. Start populating HTM using the Drupal variable.
4. Write down the `.info` file or make changes in the `.info` file of the `garland` theme as per the new theme.
5. Click on the **Clear all caches** button located at **Administration | Configuration | Development | Performance**.

Populating a Drupal theme with dynamic content (Advanced)

Before moving further, you should be aware of the meanings of Drupal variables, which are mentioned in the following section:

- A raw HTML file contains static content and using raw HTML in Drupal CMS is of no use since the powerful features of Drupal will be unexplored. To harness the powers of any CMS, the static content of HTML should be populated dynamically. Populating the content dynamically means that if the content is entered from the **Admin** panel, it should be reflected at the frontend.
- As mentioned earlier, the `garland` theme is taken as the base theme to explain things here.
- The user can also explore other default themes once he has exposure to the `garland` theme.
- The user can rename the theme as per his choice. Whatever may be the name of the theme, the `garland` theme's structure will be used and the content of the theme files will be changed as per the requirement.

▶ In the following section we will explain how to populate the Drupal theme with dynamic content, test to ensure if things are moving in the right direction, and enable the theme for testing.

How to do it...

The screenshot of the Garland theme being used as the base theme to implement instructions mentioned in this book is given in this section. Everything that will be instructed should be implemented in the PHP files of the `garland` theme.

If any other file (for example, a CSS or JavaScript file) is required to be used at any point in time, it will be mentioned specifically.

 Please remember, we will use files having the `.php` extension to populate the Drupal theme with dynamic variables. Names of the files must be intact, while the content can be changed with your HTML.

Everything we discussed until now about the `garland` theme is of no use if we don't know the location of the `garland` theme, isn't it ? How will you locate the `garland` theme? The following screenshot depicts the code structure of Drupal. Click on the `themes` folder highlighted in yellow:

Name	Date modified	Type	Size
includes	28-08-2013 09:54	File folder	
misc	28-08-2013 09:54	File folder	
modules	28-08-2013 09:54	File folder	
profiles	28-08-2013 09:54	File folder	
scripts	28-08-2013 09:54	File folder	
sites	28-08-2013 09:54	File folder	
themes	28-08-2013 09:54	File folder	
.gitignore	08-08-2013 07:34	GITIGNORE File	1 KB
.htaccess	08-08-2013 07:34	HTACCESS File	6 KB
authorize.php	08-08-2013 07:34	PHP File	7 KB
CHANGELOG	08-08-2013 07:34	Text Document	81 KB
COPYRIGHT	08-08-2013 07:34	Text Document	2 KB
cron.php	08-08-2013 07:34	PHP File	1 KB
index.php	08-08-2013 07:34	PHP File	1 KB
INSTALL.mysql	08-08-2013 07:34	Text Document	2 KB
INSTALL.pgsql	08-08-2013 07:34	Text Document	2 KB
install.php	08-08-2013 07:34	PHP File	1 KB
INSTALL.sqlite	08-08-2013 07:34	Text Document	2 KB
INSTALL	08-08-2013 07:34	Text Document	18 KB
LICENSE	18-09-2011 03:20	Text Document	18 KB
MAINTAINERS	08-08-2013 07:34	Text Document	8 KB
README	08-08-2013 07:34	Text Document	6 KB
robots	08-08-2013 07:34	Text Document	2 KB
update.php	08-08-2013 07:34	PHP File	20 KB
UPGRADE	08-08-2013 07:34	Text Document	10 KB
web.config	08-08-2013 07:34	CONFIG File	3 KB

You will be able to see the `garland` folder, as shown in the following screenshot:

Name	Date modified	Type	Size
bartik	29-08-2013 22:08	File folder	
engines	29-08-2013 22:08	File folder	
garland	29-08-2013 22:08	File folder	
seven	29-08-2013 22:08	File folder	
stark	29-08-2013 22:08	File folder	
README	08-08-2013 07:34	Text Document	1 KB

The following screenshot depicts the code structure of the `garland` theme:

color	29-08-2013 22:42	File folder	
images	29-08-2013 22:42	File folder	
comment.tpl.php	08-08-2013 07:34	PHP File	1 KB
fix-ie	08-08-2013 07:34	Cascading Style S...	2 KB
fix-ie-rtl	08-08-2013 07:34	Cascading Style S...	2 KB
garland.info	08-08-2013 07:47	INFO File	1 KB
logo	08-08-2013 07:34	PNG image	5 KB
maintenance-page.tpl.php	08-08-2013 07:34	PHP File	3 KB
node.tpl.php	08-08-2013 07:34	PHP File	1 KB
page.tpl.php	08-08-2013 07:34	PHP File	3 KB
print	08-08-2013 07:34	Cascading Style S...	2 KB
screenshot	08-08-2013 07:34	PNG image	11 KB
style	08-08-2013 07:34	Cascading Style S...	21 KB
style-rtl	08-08-2013 07:34	Cascading Style S...	5 KB
template.php	08-08-2013 07:34	PHP File	5 KB
theme-settings.php	08-08-2013 07:34	PHP File	1 KB

1. Perform the following steps to populate raw HTML with Drupal variables:
    1. Create a backup of all the files.
    2. Open a PHP file.
    3. Paste the HTML content onto the file.
    4. Replace the static text with the concerned Drupal variable.

2. Suppose a raw HTML file is having static content as given in the following code, the static content in the `head` and `title` tags will be displayed using a Drupal variable as mentioned in the preceding section using the `code [$title]` tag of Drupal.

```
[<HTML>
  <head>Our Drupal website</head>
<title>Title of the website</title>
<body>Content of the website</body>
</HTML>
]
```

3. After using the Drupal variable in our code, it should look as follows:

```
Code [
<HTML>
  <head><?php print $druapl_variable ?></head>
<title><?php print $druapl_variable ?></title>
<body><?php print $druapl_variable ?></body>
</HTML>
]
```

A list of theme variables can be found in the `garland` theme and other themes.

After populating the Drupal theme with dynamic variables, we need to test if things are working properly or not. Before that, we need to check if the `garland` theme is enabled or not. If it isn't enabled, we need to enable it

We need to perform the following steps to enable the `garland` theme (assuming Drupal 7 is installed on the user's machine):

1. Log in to the Drupal 7 **Admin** panel.

2. Enable the **Garland** theme if it is not enabled. Follow steps 3 and 4 to enable the **Garland** theme.

3. Click on **Appearance** (highlighted in yellow in the following screenshot) on the top menu bar to view a list of themes:

4. If the **Garland** theme is disabled, it will be displayed in the **Disabled Themes** section. Click on the **Enable** link to activate the Drupal theme as shown in the following screenshot:

5. Once enabled, **Garland** will appear in the **Enabled Themes** section with a message displayed as shown in the following screenshot:

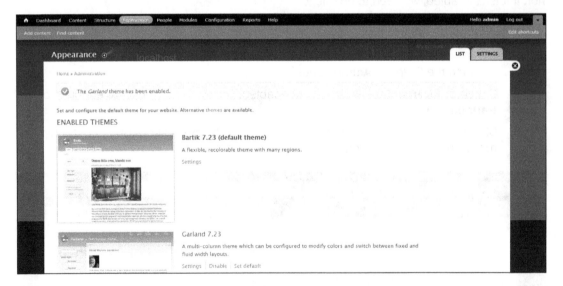

Now we are in a state where we can test if things are working properly or not. We will add content from Drupal's **Admin** panel and it should be reflected at the frontend.

We need to perform the following steps to add content:

1. Navigate to **Add content** by clicking on the **Content** tab as shown in the following screenshot:

2. Click on the **Article** link as shown in the following screenshot:

3. If the previous step is successfully executed, the page shown in the following screenshot will be opened. Enter **Title** and **Body** and save it.

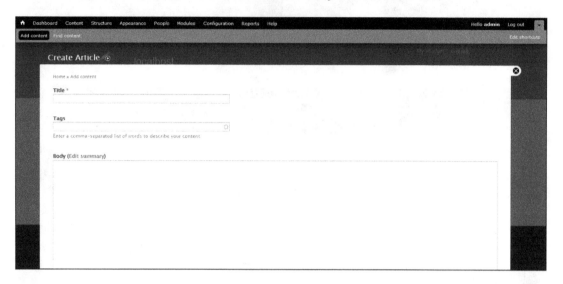

Check at the frontend. The content added by the user should be reflected at the frontend.

Theme how tos (Advanced)

Our theme name is `packttheme` for all the mentioned examples in this section.

How to do it...

Suppose our theme name is `packttheme` and we have to add three regions, namely `frontpage top`, `frontpage center`, and `frontpage bottom` on the front page. We can do it by performing the following steps:

1. Replace all occurrences of `mytheme` with the name of your custom theme.

2. Inside `themes/mytheme/template.php` (create the `template.php` file if it doesn't exist), add the following code (all the code in Drupal 5 and Drupal 6):

```php
<?php
/** Define the regions **/\function mytheme_regions() {
  return array(
        'left' => t('left sidebar'),
        'right' => t('right sidebar'),
        'content' => t('content'),
```

```
          'header' => t('header'),
          'footer' => t('footer'),
          'frontpage_top' => t('frontpage top'),
          'frontpage_center' => t('frontpage center'),
          'frontpage_bottom' => t('frontpage bottom'),
      ]
```

3. Now that the regions are defined, go to `page.tpl.php` within `themes/mytheme` and place the following code where you would like to display the appropriate regions:

```
Code [<?php if ($is_front || strstr($_GET['q'], 'admin/block')) :
?>
    <div id="frontpage_top" class="frontpage">
      <?php print $frontpage_top ?>
    </div>
    <?php endif; ?>
]
```

4. Repeat this procedure for all the three frontpage regions. You can combine two regions within one `if()` statement to improve performance.

5. To add blocks to these new regions, simply navigate to **Administer | Site Building | Blocks**.

To add a region in Drupal 7, perform the following steps:

1. Go to your theme's `.info` file and add your region in the `.info` file, for example, `[regions[packt-header] = Packt Header]`

2. Add the preceding region in `page.tpl.php`:

```
[<?php if ($page['packt-header']): ?>
    <?php print render($page['packt-header']); ?>
<?php endif; ?>
]
```

3. To add Packt Header in `node.tpl.php`, add the following code:

```
[<?php if ($page['packt-header']): ?>
    <?php print render(block_get_blocks_by_region('packt-
header')); ?>
<?php endif; ?>
]
```

4. Click on the **Clear all caches** button located at **Administration | Configuration | Development | Performance**.

The most commonly used code can be found at

https://drupal.org/node/45471

There's more...

These are some tips and advice that needs to be followed while developing Drupal.

Theme coding conventions

Commonly used coding conventions should be followed, but there are some Drupal-specific conventions that should be kept in mind while creating a theme or module.

While coding, we should prefer PHP in HTML. We should try to avoid HTML in PHP while coding templates. For example, the following coding convention should be avoided:

```
Code [<?php
if (!$page) {
  print "<h2><a href=\"$node_url\">$title</a></h2>";
}

if ($submitted) {
  print "<span class=\"submitted\">$submitted</span>";
}
?>]
```

Instead of using the preceding code, the following code should be used:

```
Code [<?php if (!$page): ?>
  <h2><a href="<?php print $node_url; ?>"><?php print $title; ?></a></h2>
<?php endif; ?>

<?php if ($submitted): ?>
  <span class="submitted"><?php print $submitted; ?></span>
<?php endif; ?>]
```

We need to separate the logic from presentation, if there is a code similar to the following one:

```
Price: Code[<?php print $price; ?>]
Tax: Code[<?php print $price * 0.075; ?>]
```

Instead of writing the preceding way, we should separate the logic from presentation as follows:

```
Code[<?php $tax = $price * 0.075; ?>]
```

Always put a semicolon at the end of all the small PHP printing statements as follows:

```
Code[<?php print $tax; ?>] - YES
Code[<?php print $tax ?>] -- NO
```

There are other coding conventions for standard Drupal coding. You can get those conventions at:

```
https://drupal.org/coding-standards
```

You can find more information about cross-browser testing at:

```
https://drupal.org/node/981614
```

You can make your theme semantically correct by visiting the following link at:

```
https://drupal.org/node/44072
```

Drupal 7 Theming Cookbook

ISBN: 978-1-84951-676-1   Paperback: 364 pages

Over 95 recipes that cover all aspects of customizing and developing unique Drupal themes

1.   Spice up your Drupal themes

2.   A complete update for Drupal 7, with added information for the Field API, Views, and Panels

3.   Part of Packt's Cookbook series with lots of practical recipes for solving the most common theming problems

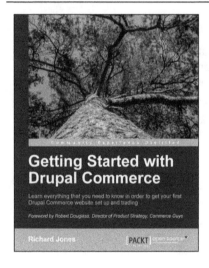

Getting Started with Drupal Commerce

ISBN: 978-1-78328-023-0   Paperback: 152 pages

Learn everything that you need to know in order to get your first Drupal Commerce website set up and trading

1.   Understand the key concepts of Drupal Commerce, its philosophy, and how it fits in the Drupal Ecosystem

2.   Learn the essentials of planning your store to save time and frustration

3.   Set up and configure your store including the catalogue, taxes, discounts, coupons, and shipping

4.   Configure your cart and checkout process and integrate them with a payment gateway

www.ingramcontent.com/pod-product-compliance
Lightning Source LLC
Chambersburg PA
CBHW060109090326
40690CB00063B/4349